7 STEPS TO IMPROVE
SELF-CONFIDENCE
FOR 8-12 YEAR OLDS

STEPHANIE LIPSEY-LIU

Copyright © 2024 by Stephanie Lipsey-Liu.. All rights reserved.
No part of this publication may be reproduced or transmitted in any form or by any means, electronic or mechanical, including photocopying, recording, scanning or otherwise, or through any information browsing, storage or retrieval system, without permission in writing from the publisher.

A note from the author

The first thing I'd like to say to you is:
You are awesome.

I know it can sometimes be hard to believe, but just know it IS true and I'm going to help YOU to see it too.

Reading this book is going to help you to realise your inner awesomeness and give you lots of tips to improve your confidence.

Sometimes we forget how amazing we are because we compare ourselves to people who SEEM better than us, or there are people in our lives who might tell us we aren't awesome.

Well, we are going to learn how to combat all of those problems and remind ourselves how great we are!

Stephanie Lipsey-Liu

Step number 1:

Positive affirmations

Positive affirmations

The first step to improving your self confidence is telling yourself how great you are. One of the ways to do this is to do positive affirmations.

What to do.
Tell yourself (out loud) how awesome you are.

How to do it.
First:
Make a list below of at least three things you want to be. (These are your affirmations.)

For example:
Amazing, funny, kind, brave, clever, smart, awesome, great, brilliant, the best.

Fill them in here:

1._____

2._____

3._____

Second:
Go and find a mirror.

Third:
Look in the mirror and say out loud:

"I am (whatever you wrote for number 1),
I am (whatever you wrote for number 2),
I am (whatever you wrote for number 3)
and I can do anything."

You can say them loudly, quietly, in a funny voice, any way you like, as long as it's OUT LOUD!

It helps if you stand up tall and smile.

This is an example of what I say:
"I am great, I am funny, I am awesome and I can do anything."

And do you know what? I actually DO believe that.

I AM great, I AM funny, I AM awesome and I CAN do anything.
If other people can't see that, I really don't mind, because only I truly know me.

Side note:
As a kid, I never said kind words to myself and I wasn't very confident and definitely didn't think I was awesome.

So you CAN change your mindset.

I know it can seem a bit odd to talk to yourself, but science has shown that telling yourself positive things out loud can actually help you believe those things.

Lastly:
Repeat, repeat, repeat.

When you wake up or when you go to bed or when you brush your teeth-choose a time to say your affirmations out loud and make it a habit.

Say them EVERY DAY!

Even if you feel silly or if you don't believe what you're saying, will you promise me you'll do it anyway? Promise me? Cross your heart?

Eventually you WILL start to believe they are true. Also, it's a good way to get used to hearing yourself talk out loud.

And that's it for tip number one!

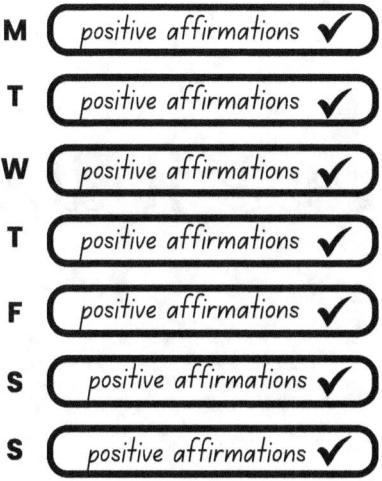

Step number 2:

Break it down

Break it down

So you want to learn something new? Break it down into small steps.

Learning anything new is HARD, so don't expect to magically be able to do it perfectly on the first try!

You are a kid, so you've got plenty of time to learn things bit by bit and make sure you get each step right before moving on to the next step.

Doing this actually helps to build your confidence.

Can you remember when you learned to read? No one gave you an adult book and said, go on then, read that! No! They taught you letter-by-letter, sound-by-sound, until eventually you could piece it all together and read confidently.

Learning to be confident is also something you should take step-by-step!

Reading this book is the first step. Trying out each of the 7 steps comes next. Then practising everything in real life is the final stage. The more you practise, the more your confidence will grow.

If you want to be good at something, start off small and work your way to the top.

It's a good idea to ask an adult to help you to work out the steps you need for whatever you want to achieve.

make a plan

Achieving each small step is a great way to improve your confidence, rather than trying to do the big thing and (probably) failing because it was too hard. That's going to make you feel bad and probably make you not want to do it any more.

These days, we see so many videos of kids who can do cool tricks or play instruments really well or are brilliant at sports. It's easy to watch and start comparing yourself to them.

However, the things you don't see are the hours and hours of practice they put in to get to that point. Or videos of when they were just starting out and they weren't very good.

Really good piano player who does hours of practice every day

This leads us to secret tip number 2 and a half: Don't compare yourself to anyone else.

Everyone is different. You don't know how much time other people have put into the things they're good at, or how much help they've had.

And you're probably forgetting that you are better than other people at other things.

There is a saying, "comparison is the thief of joy." It means, comparing yourself to others steals your happiness away!

We are all good at different things

We all have our strengths and weaknesses but we also have the power to change if we want to improve at something.

So don't get yourself down by comparing yourself to anyone else!

If someone is good at something, try and be happy for them and their achievements.

You being sad comparing yourself to an amazing dancer

You being happy doing your own thing and NOT comparing yourself to the amazing dancer

Step number 3:

Fake it 'til you make it

Fake it 'til you make it

If you PRETEND you are confident, you will eventually BE confident.

Firstly, practise making eye contact with people who are speaking to you. It shows that you are confident (even if you don't feel confident yet!) and it helps you to connect with the person talking to you.

If someone feels connected to you, they are more likely to like you. This will help your confidence grow.

Make sure you stand up straight/sit up straight too, instead of slouching. This also makes you appear confident. Practise in the mirror. If you slouch your shoulders over and put your head down, you look shy and sad and not very confident.

no slouching

stand up tall and make eye contact

Side note:

Something to be aware of (and practise) is "active listening".

When you are listening to someone, YOU know that you are listening but they don't!

Look at the person talking and nod your head if you agree with what they are saying. If you feel confident enough, you can even ask questions about what they said.

This shows them that you're DEFINITELY paying attention.

Step number 4:

Presentations

Presentations

Doing mini presentations to your family and friends is a great way to practise "public speaking."

If you're not a naturally confident person, the idea of having to speak in front of anyone can be terrifying!! Hopefully, you have someone in your family or a friend who you can practise this with.

You can even practise with a pet or a baby (if you have one handy) or just by yourself to start with.

Pick a topic that you are interested in or something that you already know a lot about.

I'll put some presentation ideas here:

sport   animals   planets   parts of the body
   cartoons   Harry Potter
super heroes   history   nature   Lego
   what happened at school   computers

If you're not sure what to start with, how about talking about something simple like colours, the alphabet, or what you can see around you? I'll give you an idea of what your presentation might sound like:

Example:
"Good morning ladies and gentlemen, today I am going to talk to you about colours. Personally, my favourite colour is yellow. It's sunny and happy and bright. Did you know, if you mix yellow with blue, you get green? Now, I'm going to tell you all the colours in the rainbow and a cool trick to remember their order. First, we have red, then orange, then yellow, then green, the blue, then indigo and finally, violet. I remember them by using the rhyme, Richard Of York Gained Battles In Vain."

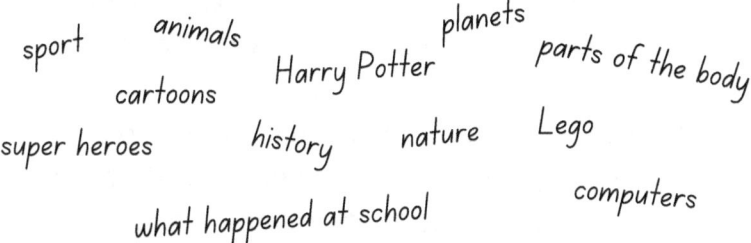

So, choosing something simple that you know about without having to concentrate too hard is a great way to practice speaking out loud.

Try and do a mini presentation every day if you can. If you want to, research and prepare a bigger presentation to do once a week. You can make notes and use them when you're doing your presentation.

If you do a presentation from paper notes, make sure you look up at your audience as much as you can, not just at the notes. (Remember, eye contact!)

It's a good idea to do some without notes so you can't hide behind them.

Also, being able to talk without any preparation is another excellent skill to have and will definitely build confidence.

Side note:

It's also a good idea to practise things that might come up in real life.

For example, what you might say in a shop:
"Good morning."
"How much is this please?"
"Thank you."

Or if you are out for a meal and you've all finished, ask your grown-ups if you can ask for the bill: (once you've practised at home!)

"Can we have the bill please?"

Talking to new people can seem scary but don't forget, they're just another human like you, going about their day. They probably won't even remember you! So, you might feel embarrassed about saying the wrong thing or stumbling over your words, but even if you do, they will move on to the next customer and not give it a second thought.

The more you practise, the easier it will get.

Have a go at pretend conversations with friends too.

"What did you do last weekend?" or
"What are you doing this weekend?"
(Don't forget eye contact and active listening when you do it in real life.)

Then, practise out loud what you did at the weekend. Keep it short for now, until your confidence grows.

Step number 5:

Join clubs

Join clubs

If you can, join a club like a drama class, a debate club, a sports club, a music group, a dance class, or Brownies/Guides/Cubs/Beavers.

Even if you aren't confident to start with, these kinds of clubs will have adults who will be more than happy to help and encourage you.

You can ask your parents to help you find a nearby club that you're interested in, or ask at school if they have any clubs you can join.

As well as doing fun activities at these clubs, it will also give you a chance to watch other children who are already confident. This can give you ideas of how to act.

Remember, fake it til you make it!

Joining a club is a great way to interact with people your own age (and older and younger too) in fun situations.

This is very different to interacting at school where you are in class, often having to work or learn quietly.

If you're not sure what kind of club to join, ask an adult to help you research clubs in your area and what they involve.

As a side note, the more things you try, the sooner you'll find something you love doing, which will naturally build your confidence.

Have a look online with an adult to see what clubs are nearby

Ideas for starting conversations at your new club when you join:

"I love your shoes/coat/bag/hairstyle! What's your name?"

"My name wasis *insert name*, what's your name?"

"Hello, I'm new here, please can you show me around?"

"Hi, I'm *your name* can I play with you?"

"Hello, I'm *your name* how long have you been at *name of club*?"

Don't forget to practise these at home if you need to.

Have a go at saying hello to new people

Ideas for things to talk about once you've made a new friend:

-Pets you have and/or pets you want
-Books you've read recently/favourite book
-Films you've seen recently/favourite film
-Hobbies
-Favourite food
-Favourite character
-What you want to do when you grow up
-Favourite subject at school
-Favourite game
-What you would do on a "yes day" (a day when your parents have to say yes to everything you ask them!)

Add some more here if you can think of any:

_____

_____

_____

_____

Step number 6:

Set boundaries

Set boundaries

You are your own person and YOU are in charge of your own body.

If someone asks you to do something you don't want to, you have the right to say NO.

For example, if someone asks you to give a relative a kiss or a hug and you don't want to, you mustn't stay quiet.

It's perfectly ok to say no.

You will need quite a bit of confidence to be able to do this but you WILL be able to do it.

Here are some options to practise:

Make sure you practise them OUT LOUD, so that when you're in an uncomfortable situation, it's easier to say them.

"No, thank you, how about a high five?"
"No, thank you, how about a fist bump?"
"No, thank you."

Sometimes, if you don't want to hug or kiss anyone, there will be time to tell your parents before it happens . Then your parents can say "give Auntie Jennie a high five," instead.

If a friend wants you to do something or go somewhere that you don't feel comfortable with, it's especially important to be able to say no.

Try practising these replies:

"No, thank you, I have to call my mum in a minute."
"No, thank you, I have to be home in 10 minutes."
"No, thank you, I don't think that is a good idea."
"No, thank you."

Don't forget, you don't have to give a reason or an explanation if you don't want to. Just be confident in your words and your body language and remember you can walk away if you need to.

It can also be a good idea to set up a code word with your parents.

If your friend asks you to do something that you don't want to do, call your parents to ask for permission but use the code word so they know you want them to say no.

For example, set it up with your parents that if you say "pretty please?" after asking, they know that that means you DON'T want to go.

Then they will tell you no, and you can blame it on your parents.

For example:

You on the phone: "Can I go to the cinema with Alex tonight? Pretty please?"

Parent: "No, not tonight, Auntie Jennie is coming to visit."

You, to your friend: "Sorry, I'd love to come but my aunt is visiting today."

Sometimes we don't feel like doing something but it's hard to say no. This way, it seems like it's your parents who won't let you go.

Step number 7:

Be kind to yourself

Be kind to yourself

Remember when we said that saying positive things about yourself makes you believe it?

Well the same goes for negative things.

If you say to yourself, I'll never be good enough, I'm stupid, no one wants to be my friend; you will actually start to believe that.

And those things are NEVER true.

Imagine if a bully was saying those things to your friend! You would stand up for your friend and tell the bully not to be so mean!

So always, ALWAYS stand up for yourself. If your inner voice EVER tells you that you're not good enough, you shut that voice up and tell it that you ARE good enough.

If you want to achieve something then you absolutely can. If you need a little help or support, that's fine!

Hold your head high and know that you truly are awesome.

Side note:

Some children will say mean things to you to try and get a reaction. Often this is because someone has been mean to them and they are taking it out on you.

The best way to deal with this, without starting to believe the things they are saying, is to imagine they said that they don't like your blue hair.

You haven't got blue hair? Well then, it doesn't affect you! You know you don't have blue hair so if they say they don't like it, then it won't bother you.

If they say you're stupid or an idiot or anything else, you KNOW that you're not those things so you can choose not to let it bother you.

This is easy for me to say but it can be really hard to do. However, it IS something you can practice.

someone being mean　　　　　　　　you not caring

Get someone you trust, like a friend or family member, to insult you. Don't forget, it's not real!

Practise any of the following in response.

"That's nice." Then walk away.
"Oh, thank you!" Then walk away.
Give them a funny look and say "Really?" Then walk away.

Other things to try that will probably confuse them are things like this:

"And you're a dinosaur!"
"And you're an apple pie!"
"And you're an umbrella!"

Use any object that is as random as possible. Don't forget to walk away afterwards!

If you can, tell a trusted adult about the situation. Like a teacher or a parent.

Try and come up with some of your own responses too.

Don't forget, eye contact and stand up tall!

Show them that you are confident enough that you don't believe what they're saying to you.

If they don't get the reaction they want, they will probably stop trying to be mean and leave you alone.

Final thoughts

I hope this book has given you some of the tools you need to help you on your way to self-confidence.

Don't forget, you don't need to be the crazy kid, the life of the party, or the joker (unless you want to). But you do need to be able to communicate what you want and stand up for yourself.

I hope this book has helped you on the way that!

Use the next few pages for writing presentations and practising your conversations.

Practice conversations

Practice conversations

Practice conversations

Presentation notes

Presentation notes

Presentation notes

Practice responses to insults

_____

_____

_____

_____

_____

_____

_____

_____

_____

About the author

Stephanie lives in Nottingham with her husband, daughter, pet dogs and pet hamster. She is an optician and a writer and loves to encourage condfidence! Stephanie loves to sing, play piano and trampoline in her spare time.

Other books by Stephanie Lipsey-Liu

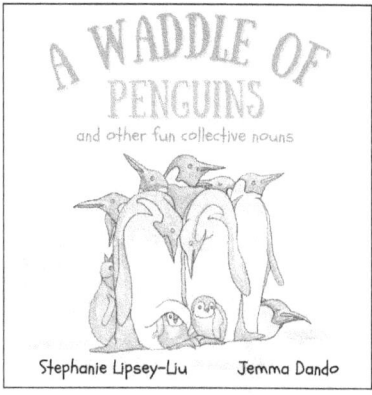

Available at
www.littlelionpublishing.co.uk

www.ingramcontent.com/pod-product-compliance
Lightning Source LLC
Chambersburg PA
CBHW072138070526
44585CB00016B/1727